LOVE! WHAT

CAGE RULE OF INDIAN PARENTS

PRIYANKA S

ISBN 978-93-5610-745-8

Published in India 2022 by Pencil

A brand of
One Point Six Technologies Pvt. Ltd.
123, Building J2, Shram Seva Premises,
Wadala Truck Terminal, Wadala (E)
Mumbai 400037, Maharashtra, INDIA
E connect@thepencilapp.com
W www.thepencilapp.com

Author biography

Priyanka S is Born in Andhra Pradesh in 2002 and grew up in the city of Chennai. The best academic performer likes to travel. The price of affection and importance is used to create both fiction and nonfiction memories in life. Her First Book has Spread the love: The Journey of Orphanage Women, 2021. Here the author says his opinion on his facts of society from both parents and children who is most struggling to get back from a broken heart. Marriage gets loved by not only two hearts it's also beloved from a blessing from all. And love always has an entity in this world.

CONTENTS

Epigraph

Does the Bride/Groom have an option or choice in selecting an alliance?

Preface

Several factors influence a woman's future financial success, on the other hand, marriage is perchance the biggest.

According to quite a few research performed in India, marriage is generally seen as a financial decision, made larger many times by the dad and mom than the achievable spouses. Among the exceptional factors in identifying marriages, caste also performs a fundamental role. In searching quite a several matrimonial advertisements, you will see achievable brides and grooms labeled by exceptional caste designations. Simply choose a newspaper and flip to the matrimonial column, and you can see the genuine nature of Indian society.

Men and girls cannot choose whom they prefer to be their partners. It is argued that there are many patriarchal explanations for that. In essence, these explanations are rooted in women's 'inferior' repute in society, which capability that their involvement in decision-making inside their family is minimal. When a man or lady chooses their companion in India, it is deemed a love marriage.

Love marriages are relatively discouraged interior Indian way of life and they symbolize a departure from organized marriages. To decide on their marriage on their own, women have to pass these interconnected hurdles.

Acknowledgements

Marriage is something that does not show up on its own. Acknowledgments enable you to thank all those who have helped in carrying out this research.

Introduction

Indian culture is never against love marriage.

All history has precious and beautiful love stories, even literature has beautiful instances of love. Parents in India still live with the outlook of controlling their adult children and love marriage is not an option. Furthermore commitment and practicality issues, parents also express concern about losing control over the child they are so madly in love with.

As a result, parents often consider their children "straying" from their family traditions when they challenge their parents' arranged marriage. In contrast to the genesis seeking Jodi and maintaining harmony with the coevals seeking Jodi, arranged marriage has been the norm around the world for centuries.

According to history, love marriages have gained a substantial amount of momentum after countless years of Shiva and Parvathi love.

Moreover, Indian Parents would compare with foreigners' love alliance, ahead they believe in Vedas in those Mahabharata and Ramayanam. Here we can be involved in seems of love, In Ramayanam, Valmiki mentioned that prince Rama and Sita love bond as loyal endure. The lesson of Generation 'The way love changes as abhorrence'.

Compared to traditional family drama, arranged marriages don't allow the boys and girls to get to know each other and directly see each other's faces after marriage. And here, I am talking about the middle-class bracket, not the higher class one. You have the opportunity to choose a partner, get to know each other, talk on the phone, and enjoy a period of courtship either. 80% of the profiles on matrimonial portals like shaadi.com or jeevansathi.com are handled by individuals in the search for their partners.

Moreover, if you believe your choice of a partner is the right one, speak up for it, and make them believe you. Moreover, they are your parents not enemies and they only want to ensure your happiness.

And if we are talking about compromises and adjustments, I would say it is a part of life. it is about adjustments in an arranged marriage and mutual understanding in love marriage.

One should be mature and responsible enough before, stepping into a relationship rather than blaming parents.

If your partner has all the merits that your parents would have liked, and they oppose the match only on grounds of caste differences, then you need not try to convince your parents. They belong to another generation, that believes fanatically in the caste system and they will never change their beliefs.

You can only make them reluctantly accept your choice by telling them that caste difference does not matter to you.

If they don’t accept, then you have two choices:

If you depend on them for support, and if you and your partner cannot survive on your own and have a separate establishment, you have no choice but to yield to their wishes.

You cannot bring a partner to live with them if they cannot accept that person on grounds of caste. Besides, it would not be fair to your partner too, to be forced to live with people who don't accept him/her on grounds of caste. You can only bring psychological pressure on them to agree by insisting you will not marry anyone else. You must wait indefinitely till they are convinced about your determination, and also about the futility of their opposition. Your partner must also be willing to wait indefinitely.

If you don't depend on them for financial support, and you and your partner are capable of living independently on your own, in your own house, you are prepared for being cut off from your own families and also risk losing inheritance and family support then you can consider informing them about your preference and decision, giving them time to adjust to it, addressing any concerns they have other than the caste differences and finally setting a deadline and then proceeding ahead by having a court marriage.

You can then only hope that Time will heal the wounds. In the future, they will come around to accepting your decision and realize that they have no choice but to move with the times. In all probability, they will. They have nothing to gain from antagonizing their children. As they grow older, they will need the support of the younger generation more than the younger generation will need the support of the older generation.

Indian parents have this weakness. They like to own their children. They have the privilege of dictating education, career, and marriage options for their adult children and taking these major decisions for their adult children instead of advising their children. By leaving the final decision up to them.

This is by allowing them to make mistakes, supporting them, and helping them recover from occasional mistakes and wrong choices. These parents may have the most sincere motives but once their children cross a certain age, they must be willing to let go. That is my humble opinion. This is not empty preaching. I have walked the talk in the matter of my own children's life, education, career, and marriage choice.

LESSON OF GENERATION

"The way love changes as abhorrence"

Since we are living in the 21st century, a lot of teenagers and adults are experiencing falling in love at first sight. We would tell this may Hormone changes but as deep they are loyal to their partner while in the relationship. As more and more men suffer while in a relationship, it is becoming more difficult to find two souls who perceive things alike.
After so many struggles in a relationship getting approval for marriage are quite difficult. To obtain permission from parents to be partners within their own family.
Yes! In India, it is quite impossible to make love between souls as with marriage. It is common for them here to get ruined with their partners, and many of them sacrifice for their families.
The generation getting increasingly large and more powerful. And Few are ready to kill their parents for their love, yes it is true. On the Other side, parents will kill their children for their social values in the caste system.
Parents have become more aware of their children's online presence in recent times. They are protected by society, yet unaware of online relationships without a mobile phone. There is no education, simply because school and college don't teach anything. The most effective way to learn is to do it yourself. Apart from this, those on the path of goals

don't even think of a relationship while parents won't even consider the idea of their children getting married. From childhood, they nourished their daughter about marriage so she could get married because physiologically she gets in the path of marriage concept. I am sure chasing marriage's conceptual theme of prolonging their children's lives destroyed them.

In contrast, parents are used to protecting their children and cherishing a good life for them. As parents pursue their self alliance, they suffer from more conditions while on a path that becomes progressively more problematic for children.

Parenthood, especially for Indian parents, can be described as a journey of thwarting prospects by being obsessively involved in every aspect of their child's growth.

PARENTING RIGHT!

Opposing love marriages is just a part of responsible parenting, for most Indian parents. Having said all that, what if you love someone —how do you convince your parents to arrange a marriage? Follow these three steps:
1) Pick someone they would approve of —Prove that your love is more than puppy love.
2) Prove your adulthood- Are you aware of the minor annoyances you create —not emptying your trousers' pockets before dumping them in the laundry hamper, not informing your whereabouts, leaving late for work perpetually, etc. Fix them. This level of self-betterment and self-cognizance shows you are maturing as a person.
3) Win over each other's family —It requires a small amount of humbleness in you to pour energy into befriending someone who views you with mistrust. It is worth it —both as a couple as well as a case -by-case.
Indian parents feel that arranged marriages are the right way for them to ensure that their children are on the right path to prosperity and happiness. Marriage reduces the significance of your parents. Fight their fears. It's crucial to prove to your family how important they are to you before even considering the issue of love marriage, and they will make your dream of a love marriage reality.

PROS AND CONS OF MARRIAGE

The following points do not apply to all 100% of cases, but the majority of cases.

LOVE MARRIAGE:

ADVANTAGES OF LOVE MARRIAGE :

You and your accomplice acknowledged every other :

You and your companion have recognized each other for years as a boy friend-girl friend which capability you to have an ample understanding of the bond you share and also about the individual you share it with, rather than going with anybody stranger. You are given your associate with her flaws and vice versa.

Even even though you and your accomplice have recognized each different for years, marriage and the relationship of a husband and a wife is completely different.

Therefore even after marriage, you may be gaining knowledge of so many new things and experiences about each different. You are aware of every other's flaws and your partner's shortcomings do not simply shock you, nor does yours surprise them. You do no longer have the stress of impressing your partner properly after marriage due to the fact they know you internally.

1. A feel of maturity:Selecting one's partner is a sign of maturity. You both have been together for so long that your conversation with each other is very robust. You both talk about problems with every different and be like 'Look this is the trouble and this is how we are going to restore it.

2. Support and security:Your accomplice helps you in every thick and thin time. You feel tightly closed when you are around them. Love, support, security, safety, and respect are what make you a family.

3. Good hygiene lifestyles :life will be first-rate as you understand your sexual desires earlier than marriage. You will get to understand their non-public hygiene, sexuality, performance, and sexual problems earlier than marriage.

4. No Shame :When you marry the man or woman you have recognized for a long time then there is no disgrace while doing romance, cuddling, or kisses. You are full because of a different person.

5. Freedom :You have the entire freedom to select your lifestyles partner. No elder or mother and father determine. You can live your lifestyle the way you want to and you select your accomplice also according to your likes and dislikes. You don't have to compromise on any ground to make your associate happy. Your associate in general loves the way you are and does no longer anticipate you to do something the way he likes. There is

freedom of thought, freedom of speech, and freedom of job in love marriage.

6. Trust :You can trust your companion as you comprehend accomplice from many months or years.

7. Love :The basis of love marriage is love. Two human beings who chose to fall in love and figure out to go for marriage. You marry any person due to the fact you love someone and no longer due to the fact you favor making others happy.

8. Free from social customs :Love marriages are no longer primarily based on the guidelines of society and so, one need not fear dowry or different social tasks.

9. Self-Satisfaction :In a love marriage, you feel self-satisfaction that you have married a character with whom you wanted to marry. You don't do any be apologetic about in future that I desired to marry a character whose I loved very lots but I may want to now not do. You feel the satisfaction I have married my cherished one.

DISADVANTAGES OF LOVE MARRIAGES:

1. You will be in a distinct world. You cannot see whatever logically, however only emotionally (love/attraction/lust)
2. Emotions will fade away after a few months after marriage and you will recognize practical

existence (then you will take note of your mother and father's words)

3. If your existence is as you expected, it will be fine. Else fights will happen.
4. Risk of dad and mom now not agreeing to be given the marriage and even killing for status (in case of inter-caste marriages).
5. If both are working, the an extra risk of divorce.
6. Risk of dropping all household if marry against dad and mom consent.
7. Risk of becoming an orphan if accomplice cheats after marriage (for girls)
8. It will be tough when children are born when there is no lady help for the girls.
9. Once in existence time you will feel no longer solely love, but different family members are also essential in life.

Conclusion :

Love marriage is no longer the standard to be happy, " love in marriage" is.

ARRANGE MARRIAGE
ADVANTAGES OF ARRANGED MARRIAGE:

1. People may additionally suit better:Since family contributors or different expert matchmakers pick a partner for the bride, there would possibly be a greater hazard than these humans fit with every different because they would possibly share similar views on the world and might have the same goals in life.Therefore, if experienced family participants

search for an appropriate partner, the chances that the suit between the married couple will be pretty first-rate may increase.

2. The higher stage of the trip for parents :Since parents have lots greater lifestyles trip than their kids, they might additionally be higher capable to determine which accomplice would possibly be healthy for their girl or their boy and which would not.Hence, it ought to make the experience that parents get concerned in the choice procedure involving practicable life companions in view that they often are aware of their adolescents quite well and often comprehend what's proper for them (or at least they assume they do)

3. Assurance of social status:Arranged marriages regularly additionally have the gain that they can assure an excessive social status.For instance, in many countries, mothers and fathers strive to find an accomplice for their son or their daughter which has an excessive social status so that their young people can marry up and have a higher social status themselves, which is frequently also interpreted as a greater ordinary high-quality of life.

4. Financial security:There is additionally an economic component when it comes to marriages.Many marriages, particularly arranged marriages, are now not executed due to love, but due to the truth that one accomplice wishes to improve his or her wealth level.This was the norm

as a substitute than the exception solely one century ago and till now, the monetary element associated with marriages is pretty important.

5. Cultural similarities of partners:Another benefit of organized marriages is that companions regularly have pretty similar backgrounds and cultural values.Most often, dad and mom select partners for their youngsters that have comparable cultural values so that they will also suit well into the family.Similar values additionally make it greater probably that the marriage works out in view that there might be fewer conflicts between the partners in the long run.

6. Rational as a substitute for an emotional decision:In general, organized marriages usually come from a rational standpoint and feelings do now not play a role at all. This can be viewed as both fine and negative.The wonderful component of rational choices related to marriage is that all the special aspects humans are getting into are considered from a goal standpoint and additionally all the risks can be evaluated better.Therefore, arranged marriages may additionally lead to higher decisions and a higher average great of lifestyles for the respective companions compared to marriages that are primarily based on love and feelings rather than on difficult facts.

7. Family connections are strengthened:Another upside of arranged marriages is that the connection between extraordinary households can

be bolstered quite a lot.In many cultures, the connections between households are pretty essential in all areas of daily lifestyles and good connections to family members may additionally be beneficial when it comes to future professional prospects.

8. Similar ethics:Arranged marriages make it also more in all likelihood that humans have equal ethics because they frequently come from similar cultural backgrounds and have been taught identical matters when they had been young.Thus, due to these comparable ethical perspectives, the chances for a marriage that works out, in the long run, might be higher.

9. Religious fits:Arranged marriages may also make it additionally extra probable that human beings fit on a nonsecular level.Since mother and father will actively search for partners with similar backgrounds, the nonsecular fit can be assured, and therefore, it might additionally be extra possibly that companions get along with every different because they may share an identical attitude towards religion and existence in general.

10. Similar values:In general, companions that met each other due to organized marriages are quite likely to share similar values for the reason that their mother and father make sure that the cost of the companion will shape the family values to assure a peaceable and harmonic coexistence.

11. People may stay in a completely happy bubble:Even even though people who had been pressured into arranged marriages will in no way have the probability to actively date different partners, they may nevertheless live in a certain variety of bubbles.Since they are in no way skilled in the excitement of dating, they will additionally not comprehend what they are missing out on, and therefore, those people might stay in a type of completely happy bubble and might even be happier than accept this arranged marriage construct.

12. Avoidance of lovesickness:Another gain of organized marriages is that people can additionally avoid feeling lovesickness.Many people around the world may additionally get quite damaged due to a breakup with a partner and may also go through serious emotional pain.Yet, via organized marriages, this problem will be long past considering that there will now not be the opportunity to search for an accomplice, and therefore, the possibility of lovesickness is also eliminated.

13. No stress to discover a partner:Finding an appropriate associate may additionally be quite a task for many human beings all over the world.Our expectations are regularly quite excessive and we will consequently regularly journey disappointments throughout the dating process.In contrast, with an arranged marriage, there is no stress to discover and vet a companion

because your mother and father or other matchmakers will do the job for you.

DISADVANTAGES OF ARRANGED MARRIAGES

1. Love is frequently not a factor:As we have considered before, arranged marriages can have some advantages.One drawback of organized marriages is that love will most often be no longer a component at all.Maybe partners may also get alongside with every other, however, they will probably never have any form of feeling for each other.This can be regarded as pretty sad because many human beings marry because they have strong emotions for each other and enjoy their time together and organized marriages will now not account for this important element at all.

2. There can also be no suit at all between partners:Even though there will possibly not be love worried at all, humans may nevertheless get along with each other.Yet, in many organized marriages, now not even this will be the case.Most often, this sort of bonding will turn out to be a real mess and companions will frequently have disputes.After a certain while, some partners will frequently just resign and just match the needs and needs of the different accomplices to keep away from serious trouble.

3. Potential greater divorce rates:Depending on the use of a and on the man or woman circumstances, arranged marriages would possibly additionally lead to greater divorce rates. Even if this is not the

case, some companions can also truly get away from their marriage with the aid of journeying to foreign nations with hopes for a higher existence to get out of their misery.Moreover, even if humans continue to be in organized marriages, many of them might now not be joyful at all.

4. Separation may additionally be difficult:It will frequently also be pretty hard to get out of an arranged marriage because households are regularly bonded pretty tight together and if you favor leaving a marriage, you will also have to cut all cords to all your family members.This would possibly be too painful for many partners and therefore, they frequently figure out to stay in a marriage as an alternative than to quit it given that they fear the penalties that would be applied via divorce.In many cultures, divorce is additionally in opposition to religious beliefs and human beings who wreck up might also have to fear serious punishment.

5. Spouses may additionally not believe every other:Since they sincerely do not comprehend every difference before the marriage takes place, there may additionally be a vast lack of trust between companions in marriage.Hence, if partners do no longer have faith in each other, it might be quite hard to maintain a working marriage given that distrust can break bonds between partners.

6. People may be quite unhappy:In general, humans who are forced into arranged marriages may additionally be lots unhappier compared to human beings who were capable to choose their accomplice via themselves because they may experience like all the freedom of preference had been taken away from them and they never had any effect on this essential existence decision.

7. Family problems: Since companions are not in a position to choose whom they favor marrying, organized marriages regularly also lead to serious household problems.Quite often, there is stress on a daily groundwork between partners, which may additionally flip into serious disputes in the lengthy run.Yet, human beings would possibly be too afraid to destroy up and to start a new existence with a distinct accomplice and may nonetheless stay in their misery due to this excessive level of fear.

8. No room for personal choices: Personal desire concerning such necessary topics as marriage is regarded to be a human right in many regions of our planet for an essential reason.However, in international locations the place organized marriages are the norm, there is no room for non-public preference, and this essential human proper is frequently entirely taken away from people.

9. Husband and wife might also have no say: In fact, in arranged marriages, partners frequently have no say at all when it comes to deciding on their future

wife or husband. Instead, they often have to solely matter on matchmakers or on household individuals to make this essential desire for them.Even if they are not attracted to their future associate at all, human beings would possibly actually have no preference other than to agree to the marriage to keep away from serious trouble with their family members.

10. May promote gender inequality :Another drawback of organized marriages is that they might also considerably contribute to gender inequality.Women frequently have an awful lot fewer rights compared to men in these organized marriages and therefore, they may get trapped in those organized pair-bonding situations.This can also additionally lead to a state the place females will not be allowed to get any sort of education and their lives can also flip out into a mess due to that considering they will continually be dependent on their husbands, which is in no way appropriate thinking considering that it leads to an imbalance of electricity in a relationship.

11. People regularly don't be aware of what they are getting into:Even though many people assume that complying with the rules of getting into an arranged marriage is the proper factor to do since they are instructed to do so with the aid of their family and friends, those marriages tend to turn out into nightmares and people can also realize too late what they have gotten into.Therefore, humans can also additionally not be aware of the

genuine consequences of these arranged marriages, which might also lead to serious troubles later on in their lives.

12. Dating length can also be lacking in a couple's life: Many of us also virtually experience courting many extraordinary people till we discover the accomplice that excellent matches our preferences.However, it is only feasible to figure out who suits us if we get skilled in dating.Hence, if this ride is missing, plenty of enjoyment is taken out of all of it and also, the probability of a misfit will end up a great deal higher.

13. Emotional stress :Marrying and spending your life with the wrong associate may additionally also mean plenty of emotional stress.I could no longer even think about living with an accomplice I don't like an awful lot and spending my whole existence with such an individual would make me sense quite sad.This may also flip into plenty of emotional stress and different problems in the long run.

14. Lower existence expectancy :People in forced marriages might additionally go through a substantially lower existence expectancy.It has been demonstrated by way of much research that people who experience dwelling with a partner will have a drastically higher life expectancy than human beings who are depressed with their partners or who have no partner at all.Therefore, arranged marriages may additionally also do

human beings no favor in phrases of common existence expectancy.

15. Confined stage of freedom :Freedom is a treasured human right and the confinement of freedom thru arranged marriages should be viewed to be quite problematic.In fact, in my opinion, everything that takes away our freedom has to be regarded to be intolerable, and only in a few rare cases, this confinement in freedom can be justified.Therefore, because pressured marriages take away the freedom of people, they never are the norm.

16. Child marriages :Another problem with arranged marriages is that baby marriages grow to be a good deal greater likely.Children get regularly married at a pretty young age and will have no danger at all to get away from this construct.In turn, being a baby for a positive length of time is truly taken away from those children, which might also result in plenty of emotional issues in the lengthy run.

17. Mental issues :There will additionally be lots of mental issues associated with organized marriages.Even though it can not be measured by way of research considering that many humans in pressured marriages are truly too afraid to document their intellectual prerequisites and their misery to the backyard world, it is estimated a high fraction of humans in arranged marriages suffer from sizable depression and different intellectual issues because they are frequently clearly not

capable to deal with the fact that they essentially have to waste their lifestyles entirely to comply with the needs of their families.

WHY INDIAN PARENTS ARE AGAINST LOVE MARRIAGE

They are afraid of going through non secular and cultural troubles if they allow their teenagers to do love marriages. It is very hard to regulate a boy or girl who does no longer belongs to their caste or religion. They are afraid of other family individuals and human beings around them who say about their child marrying anyone who belongs to every other religion. It is very challenging to stay in society except for the cooperation of people around them. They don't want to lose the popularity of their household by way of marrying anyone who doesn't belong to their religion/caste. Indian parents believe that it is better to die than to enable their youth to marry a boy/girl from any other caste/religion. Indian parents suppose that they only have the proper to choose a perfect companion.

This book consent to the author's appreciation of Indian cultures of psychology being pushed using a girl or boy whilst it comes up in a selection of a lady or boy's life.

Personally experienced on the center type as nicely us rich class family content material that, he or she won't have the expertise to take up a decision as a substitute of they (parents or household members) proper to predict they life.

DOWRY IS A FEE

FOR NOT GETTING A MARRIAGE

90% organize marriages depend on dowry. Give them cash and take happiness for lifestyles time. All in the organized marriage is about money. I usually saw one component 90% arrange marriages humans have a stressful life. Many organize married housewives are now not doing the jobs if housewives are now not happy and they wanna a divorce. They can not divorce because where they will carry money to supply food, garments, and education. So they have to manage. nowadays many humans are against female toddler training and job. They supply their woman childless training like eighth passed, fifth passed and 10 passed it's now not ample to do a nice job and supply your infant a better life. Maybe the housewife has divorced then their parents forget about them because she did not undergo his husband and husband's family abuses. But it's now not about all the families. Only 90% of human beings are struggling with it.

It is now not quintessential to recognize what this might also be regarded as. What is integral is whether you are happy with your decision. If you are content with your decision, you will no longer be troubled about what humans think about you to be. You will be strong ample to face the consequences and repercussions from society.

Just think about each scenario.
1. You are married to the one you love. It's a pleasant life, but you pass over your mother and father sometimes. You leave out the love of your mom and the aid of your father. Maybe they will come to receive you and your beloved over time, maybe not. But how essential is their acceptance or rejection to you? That is the principal point. Are you ok with the reality that they might also even now not take delivery of your wedding ever?
2. You are married to anyone else for your dad and mom's happiness. Your mother and father are quite joyful with the marriage, but can you imagine yourself being married to any person other than the one you love? If your heart says it is not adequate then perhaps you have to go with the aid of your heart. Do you assume you can live happily with this other character without the one you loved haunting your thoughts? If you suppose you can manage to forget the one that you love now then possibly you should go with the marriage for your parents' happiness
3. If you are without a doubt certain about your love, I think you must go and marry that person. It is my opinion and I might be wrong, but I assume mother and father don't have the right to manage their children's lives or choices.

Parents solely have the duty of loving, cherishing, and offering to their children. They are not given to determine what their young people can and cannot do in life.

If your mother and father are now controlling your desire in one of the most important factors of your life, they will proceed with their control after your marriage, if you marry as per their wishes.

On the different hand, going using your heart and

marrying the love of your existence will also be a way of displaying to them that they can no longer control you. It also shows that you no longer want their support and they may also withdraw it as well. But you have to understand that their guide probably comes mixed with control. It's your choice to make.

If you suppose you can just now not manage except for your parent's assistance and approval, maybe you must start questioning how healthy your relationship with your parents is.

That being said, I would additionally like to point out that going in opposition to your dad and mom ought to motivate other participants of your family to take sides. Your relationship with your siblings and/or aunts and uncles could change significantly. They may additionally overtly guide you or criticize you. If you understand someone in your household who married in opposition to your mother and father's wishes, it would do properly to think about how your family took it.

Remember, even if things do not go well, you will have the right lesson for life. A decision may be desirable or bad, however in no way wrong. A suitable selection gives you happiness while a terrible one offers you lessons and existence experience. You can continually find happiness in existence even after a terrible decision. So don't be afraid to go using what you feel.

On the whole what matters is, what is of high significance to you. This is one of the most important selections of your existence and you have to make it neither in haste nor going by using the words of any person else. Think it out good and decide. Your whole existence after marriage depends on it and make certain you do not regret your decision.

I will cease now pronouncing that most instances your coronary heart tells you what you want and it will do good to listen even if your head can not recognize what it says. So if your heart is stolen, hand it over legally to that thief who stole it. Go in advance and marry your love. Trust your heart. This could cease up being the exceptional choice of your life.

When the boy asks for something from a girl's family it's called dowry but what about the girl's family expecting too much from the boy & his family. Reverse dowry?

PARENTS FEARS MARRIAGE ENDS IN DIVORCE!

DID SO ARRANGED?
PARENTS FEARS MARRIAGE
ENDS IN DIVORCE!
Just the fact a marriage does now not end in divorce does now not suggest it is successful.
In India, many factors play the foremost position in so-called successful arranged marriages.

How can people who didn't marry using their very own choice, can locate the power to separate via their choice

In most cases of arranged marriages, people marry due to the stress of parents, society, relatives, etc. They additionally continue to be married because of the stress by way of these people.

1. Women are not impartial in our country

It is said that many girls in our u . s . are not working. Some ladies are pressured to stop working after they get married. They are financially established with their husband. They are scared about how they will control the entirety on their own.

2. Custody of the child(ren)

In some cases, human beings are scared that they will lose custody of children. They are afraid that they won't be able to see their youngsters ever again. People are unaware of family legal guidelines in India.

3. Abusive Marriages

People in abusive marriages are scared of leaving their partners. The fear is deep-rooted in their mind. They are continually scared of their companion abusing them. They don't even approach any legal professional using themselves, as they don't understand what their companion will do when they discover out.

4. Comfort Zone

Some humans emerge as comfy with their marriage. Even when it is no longer good. Some human beings discover their marriage higher than many different marriages. They don't choose to step into an unfamiliar situation. They just let it be. Some think that their marriage is not good, but it's not horrific either.

5. Divorce is a terrible thing

In India, people choose a divorced person. Divorce is viewed to be an uncultured practice in India. People are usually taught to adjust.

Many love marriages don't certainly love marriages

All the human beings who had love marriages weren't necessarily in love. Many human beings think they are in love when they aren't. They never lived collectively before. They marry because they desire to stay together.

WHY DOES A LOVE MARRIAGE GET MORE DIVORCES

The divorce rate of love marriages may be greater than that of arranged marriages but you can't say arranged marriages are more successful than loved ones.

It's just that in arranged marriage there is pressure from parents to continue with the marriage otherwise what society would think and in that 99% of the success of marriages is dependent on the ability of women to change and compromise. If that's not there, it results in divorces. But if the marriage is arranged the major point is you are bound to make compromises on both ends, it's understood.

Now coming to love, look you may be for years in love with someone, but staying with them for 24 hours and with your in-laws sometimes may prove nagging. Couples are not ready for that, moreover, the psychology is he/she knows me very well so why should we change. And here is where the flaw lies. Marriage is a very big commitment. But when you start to take each other for granted, for some time it's worth giving it a try as you are madly in love but for how long.

As a result, distances start to creep in and eventually the end of the marriage.

So the first component of any kind of marriage is to have a

mutual understanding and the will to make compromises. And any marriage can be a success then.

Indeed, 90% of love marriage does not succeed, but Not all love marriages like this.

Be it love marriage or arrange marriage to play both Need to love, care Understanding. These three words are very important to make Succeed in married life.

Since the couple knows each other before marriage, the expectations from each other are much more than that in an arranged marriage. This especially rings true for the wife since after a fairy tale romance every girl expects a happily ever after. She expects her husband to support her over his parents which rarely happens. The husband, on the other hand, rarely will stand for his wife against his parents (even when it is obvious that their behavior is wrong) since he has already disappointed them by marrying a girl of his choice and won't commit the blasphemy to support her over them.

The promises and assurances that the couple makes to each other in their courtship period aren't always kept. People change after marriage, the mask falls off and only the reality remains. It hurts because you marry that person because of those promises and therefore you expect him to keep his word. When it doesn't happen, the disappointment sets in.

Contrary to an arranged marriage, very few material things (job, money, education, position) matters in love marriage. The alliance is based more on emotions(love, care, support). If these emotions change, it becomes very difficult to compromise on that front. The compromises over material things are willingly made in love

marriage but when it comes to an emotional compromise,

the relationship breaks.
In-laws play an important role in breaking a love marriage. Since the girl is not of their choice they don't hesitate to highlight her flaws to their son.
Intercaste love marriage is even more difficult especially if you are living in a joint family setup. Their caste, her caste, their rituals, her rituals, their food, her food, the list goes on. the ones of responsibility fall on the husband's shoulders in a love marriage since he married the girl of his choice and brought her into his household, amongst his people. I don't
It's the reverse. Arranged marriage ask husbands to blindly support their wives, but to apply their wisdom and logic and take a stand for the betterment of their spouse, children, and extended family.

ALSO IN SOME CASES:

Arrange Marriages have the highest divorce rate and the rate is very regional as well. The primary reason is dowry. Dowry is rampant in North and South India, it's a big leveler in keeping the couple in control, hence in North India it's seen that people in love marriages, where there is no dowry, it's easier for them to file a divorce. In Bengal, Orissa, Delhi city arranged marriages have a higher divorce rate, there is no or minimum dowry culture in these regions, parents are very supportive of girls, and most women even after marriage receive at least an apartment from their parents as heir, it is also a city where women are safe and judged for not being married or divorced, hence divorce rate is higher for arranged marriages in East India. I have personally witnessed this in my neighborhood, friend circle, and relatives.

SOCIETY ACCEPTANCE

Even though the whole world accepts changes happening in our society India has not changed yet. The main example that proves it is the take of Indian parents towards love marriage. They don't accept love marriages easily. There are some traditional and ritual beliefs going on in India even now. Indian parents very much believe in them and they are afraid of society and the people around them. Caste and religious systems are existing in that society even now and they want to marry their daughter or son in the same caste and religion.

Many Indian Hindu parents check matches between the birth chart of a boy and a girl before proceeding with marriages. If the matches and free from any doshas in the future, then only they will proceed with that relation. This is a belief of Indian parents that astrology can solve all their problems and it is true also.

BEST WAY OF CHOOSING A PARTNER

1. Laughter:
   Find someone that not only laughs at your humor and quirks but doesn't take life too seriously. Laughter can solve many worthless arguments.

2. Support:

   Find someone that has your back 99.999% of the time. They will address issues in private and not in public.

3. Attraction:

   Looks aren't everything, but initially, they get the ball rolling. If you find someone that you find highly attractive and their mind matches that, there's your answer.

4. Communication:

   Find someone that will hurt you with honesty but not destroy you with betrayal and lies. Find that person that can and will talk about the uncomfortable situations that will come up throughout the relationship.

5. Personality:

   Find someone that has open-minded, and nonjudgmental similar to yours.

6. Availability:

   Find someone who is available. Physically, mentally and emotionally. They don't make you "guess" what their intentions are. You don't have to chase or "guess" what is going on.

7. Interested:

   Find someone interested in "your" life, as well as has a life of their own. There's give and take on both sides.

8. Intimacy:

   Find someone who matches your level of intimacy. Sex isn't most important, but it does play a big role at least for me.

9. Constructive Criticism:

   Find someone that will give you the criticism that will help you achieve a better version of yourself.

10. Acceptance:

    Find someone who accepts you exactly as you are. They offer support but won't try and change you. What they see is what they get. Don't confuse this with accepting abusive behavior.

11. Awareness:

    Find someone aware enough to know, that relationships aren't easy. No one is perfect and there is no "perfect" match. This person will understand everyone, and life, in general, is a work in progress. It's all about progress, not perfection.

12. Hug:

    Find a person whose hug changes a complete shit show of a day into a ray of sunshine

13. The look:

    Finally, find that person that looks at you and has a way of meeting you. Someone that will look at you, with no words, but the look says "Don't worry, I got you."The bottom line, there's no guaranteed way to choose a "life" partner. People change, that's a fact of life. What two people find attractive at first can lead to what destroys the relationship in the future.Your best bet is making choices on how you want to spend the rest of your life with "yourself." And if someone comes along with the same goals and plans as yours, take it slow and see where it goes

KEEP IN MIND WHILE CHOOSING A WOMAN AS A WIFE

"To get what you want, you have to deserve what you want. The world is not yet a crazy enough place to reward a whole bunch of undeserving people."
— Charles T. Munger

Create A Powerful Vision for Yourself
Write down values, qualities, or attributes that you want in an ideal woman. To give you an example, here are some values you look for in a woman.

- Health
- Continuous Growth
- Authenticity/Genuineness
- Contribution
- Humility
- Compassion
- Humor

Once you have a list, rank them in the order of importance from one to ten with ten being the most important.

This is the deal maker list. It's equally as important to list out your deal-breakers.

Because a woman who values her health is most important. Secondary criteria include your lifestyle compatibilities such as views on marriage, children, and locations to live.

These are important topics to discuss and align in the early stages of the dating process before you fully invest in her.

Now that you have defined your dream woman, here comes the most difficult part.

You must become the person that embodies all those values, traits, or attributes. That's because a woman who has all those qualities you listed wouldn't want to be with a man who also doesn't have similar characteristics.

You must be a high-quality man to attract and keep a high-quality woman. You may be able to use gimmicky tricks or fancy gadgets to attract the woman. Sooner or later, she will know your true character.

Besides, those women who you do attract with money aren't the ones you want to be with. You may want to be with them because of their goddess-like physical features. But that will fade with time and you won't be interested in them because of your lack of emotional connection with them.

It's best not to invest time and energy in those types of women.

To attract and keep your ideal compatible women, you must present your best authentic character. Of the values, qualities, or attributes that you have written down, put next to them a score of one to ten with ten being the highest - meaning you're completely in love with it and there's no

room for improvement.
Be 100% honest with yourself because this is only for your eyes. No one is going to see it unless you choose to share it.

Create An Action Plan
Now that you have a vision of what you want in a woman, it's time to create an action plan to become the man she wants.

How will you become that man with all the values, qualities, or attributes you have created for yourself?
What steps will you take to become that man?

Get realistic and specific, then start small, that way you will build momentum and confidence as your progress.
For example, if you want to be funnier, identify what type of humor you like. Then surround yourself with more of those types of comedy by watching videos, listening to audio, or reading books on that topic.
After consuming the appropriate knowledge, you must go out and practice implementing what you have learned with family members, friends, or strangers.
Regardless of what skill you're working on, appreciate the small wins because over time they add up to big victories.
If your strategy isn't working, listen to the feedback and adjust accordingly. Consistently work on yourself while you go out and meet people, especially women.
As a man, you must take the lead and initiate every interaction with the opposite gender. Put yourself out there and talk to anyone and everyone so that it becomes a habit

for you to meet new people daily

After building a strong rapport with new friends, exchange contact information so you can invite them to future events. Use your outings as a filtering process to select high-quality men and women for your life.

Be consistent with it and eventually you'll have an abundant social circle with both high-quality men and women. Because high-quality people tend to have high-quality friends, you can use it as a method to meet high-quality women.

During this arduous journey, you will face many inevitable "failures" and "rejections." Don't give up because this is all part of the process.

If necessary, ask for help from close friends and mentors because they want to help you succeed. Understand those struggles are there to challenge you and make you stronger. They're there to make your story deeper and more powerful. Therefore, embrace all the obstacles, hardships, and adversities.

One day you'll look back and be thankful for them. Because without those defeats, you wouldn't be the man you are today.

Don't Ever Settle

You know you're settling when you compromise any of the values, qualities, or attributes on your deal maker list.

When you deserve less than what you want in your romantic relationship, you and your woman both suffer. That's because deep down, you believe you desire someone better.

As a result, you won't be able to fully give yourself to her.

Apathetic about your woman, you eventually will seek

excitement elsewhere. This might even result in having affairs with other women.

Your partner deserves your best. Not being able to give that to her, you're "cheating" her chance of being with a man who can. This isn't fair to either of you.

Both of you deserve someone who truly thinks you're the best compatible person in the world for them. You both win when you two want and deserve each other.

Become a Chooser

As scary and lonely as it may sound, you're better off being alone than being with the wrong woman. With constant external pressure from parents, friends, and society, you're extremely tempted to give in and settle. But the price you pay is an unhappy life with an incompatible partner.

Do you truly want that?

Is it worth all the trouble and hassle of settling which will result in inevitable unhappiness and possible divorce?

The fear of being alone forever is real.

That's why you must start your life-transformation journey now. Put in the work now so you can bear the fruits later.

Nothing meaningful will come easy because you're not entitled to anything. Believe in yourself and become the man women want.

Your dream partner is out there improving on herself and she can't wait to meet you.

She won't show up until you're ready. And one day, your paths will cross.

Epilogue

The way I concluded is that I heard Sadhguru in a video talking about this debatable topic of Arranged marriage or Lover marriage and has said that, all marriages are arranged irrespective of us or somebody. So it does not matter if parents are arranging it, a commercial website is arranging it, or a dating app, local bar, confused friend, or confused self! Anyway, it is an arrangement.

So, God's dictates are not able to stop the breakups. Law is not able to stop the breakups. You need to understand this when parents organize, you must, I'm asking you a basic question. Do you believe, their judgment may not be the best, but parents have your best interest of yours. But if you have matured beyond them, that's different. You can make your own decisions. But, arranged marriage is the wrong terminology. All marriages are arranged. By whom, is the only question. I think it should be arranged by people who are most concerned about your well-being. Who has a larger reach, because you can't find the best man or the best woman in the world. Because we don't know where the hell they are.

So I have concluded after listening and reading, If we are more mature than our parents and are more responsible for ourselves having a vision that we are marrying for ourselves and that we need the person rather than they need us, it can be arranged that way too with further support and guidance. Hence, All marriages are arranged and let us decide with a lot of responsibility as whoever it is arranged by.

Notes

Task:
Furthermore, If you want to ask or discuss ,Come forward…
Mention us on social media, and
Drop your review at Kindle/ amazon/ flipzat
Write me a view point @mail

To Reach:
Email: priyankasrinivasulureddy@gmail.com
Instagram Id: @priyankasrinivasulureddy
Twitter ID : priyanka312402

www.ingramcontent.com/pod-product-compliance
Lightning Source LLC
LaVergne TN
LVHW050425160726
843469LV00041B/1223

9789356107458